DARLING ANGEL MEAT

Poems by Kate Robinson

Shoe
Music
Press

Cover design by Katie McCarthy

Thank you for your support and that of poetry in
general.

Table of Contents

Imitation Silver Reasonably Priced
Wine Opener 1

Belly fat, not child. 2

after hours, off the cross 4

rats in the grass *or drunk texting 5

Priority 6

Lay Down Memorial 8

Soda-jerk 9

He had a huge scar across his back 10

Girls driving chariots 11

That angel wasn't back-lit 12

the withdrawal method 13

Jackie's Oh- face 14

A Woman Sold Spices 15

What to remember when walking
behind a woman. 17

*They are drawn to the light,
not the neck* 18

Ugly little life 20

In the deer body 22

what that becomes 23

Illegotcka 25

I climb you 26

emotional hemophiliac 27

Pub Sow 28

Acknowledgements 29

Imitation Silver Reasonably Priced Wine Opener

I screw the head, push with each rotation.
The levers rise as if to praise.
I push hard, extract the woody stopper,
open the body of opening.

I'm going to kneel and think quietly: I miss you.
The vine I thirst for isn't
on the tongues of the righteous.
The stomach is embittered to want.

I want to see my father— who is alive
and has two new children
he will not live to see graduate.
Angry highways across his nose

deliver oxygen to the extremities.
My wine is cheap. That's what I can afford.
I will need more of it
to begin the unfeeling.

Belly fat, not child.

I dream of slicing it open a bit, to see the yellow
cell quilt
I've been building for years.

I like the way my breasts are pessimistic.
The way I hoist and pulley myself with
affordable cotton masonries—

scaffolding— corporeal marionettes to defy any
lost epidermal elasticity;

to increase, augment, minimize something in my
nature.
Despite the initial swelling, and renovations—
breasts are built to fall.

Jug band body, upholstered trunk,
I'll run in heavy legs grateful for the blood.

Every labored breath pushes death back an inch.
No machine will hold open

my lids long enough to see what happens
afterwards so
I'll carry this soft engine for hours. I'll run a mile
for each year

of my life, and it won't be pretty. I'll sit in an ice
bath after,
and imagine slicing open my IT bands, taut e's on
a violin.

I dig into my legs with my knuckles to ease the
burden of hips,
pluck the steady ribbon of corpse. The shower is
a daily humiliation.

Stall of wonders, a place for discovery.
When I am dry I will find the Vitamin I, B
(profin.)

A single glass of $9 merlot. A microwave
high fiber lady-dinner. The television.
I step out looking paler and vulnerable
my hair a thin river—
This body, Dresden.

after hours, off the cross

when we would pour cheap vodka
into the paper cups we had been filling with
coffee all day
when we could choose what music we were
listening to
and the aprons came off and we shared
closing duties, who would mop— who cleaned
the bathrooms
who restocked, who counted the drawers
who scrubbed the enormous scalding vats,
baskets that dripped all brown

Foods that were left over were split among us,
what we couldn't bear to eat, the pastries whose
scent had become
a Pavlovian response for a wasted life,
to hours that were not ours—
we put them in a paper bag
blueberry bread, bran muffins, cookies almost
stale
and left outside for the homeless

some days we'd walk together to the train, the
bus
most days we would go to a bar near by, and
watch others
getting ready to close their kitchens
we'd drink heavy and fast
we'd tip well
then home to shower,
the smell of coffee would brew off our skin
and down the drain
how you take your coffee says
too much about you

rats in the grass *or drunk texting*

ats on ourwalk ho me 4rm the bar
the nite b4 I finallygav e up the monstr
the nite b4 i strtd 2 requ ire a tv on 2 sleep

rats, if u spit ona dumpstr will cumout in2the
prking lot
nd u can c 'em doin their ra tty thing

iwas telin u wht 2 read nxt

 nd u were sying goeasy, easy there
woahgrl, easy   sugr cube?

N'dall isaw
was theglass mybigsistrfell in2
tearing off agud 7" ofhertanned elbw4armskin

rats in the grass patches minicityyards lookin on
as ilicked herwound
nd we let ourheadsbak nd we lafd up sum sad-
magi c

Priority

and then you thought
finally I can just eat some ice cream

in peace
although

trying to hold the spoon is difficult
when you're bleeding all over your hands

and your ankles are still tied together—
but the man and his wife

have left you to your own devices
at least for a few godly hours

and that is your reward for all
the days, maybe even weeks of good behavior

and with your chaffed wrists you can pry open
the freezer
or the front door

at least you know what's behind one of them
and so you set about breaking the padlock on the
freezer door

with the man's hammer
he left right next to your cot

you swing at the thing
and it breaks on the first try

and when the icy smoke spills from that
sacred box, you can see the kelly green of the
thin-mints

purchased from roving gypsies months ago
and the silvery sheen of the cubic 6 pack—

what wouldn't you do for a Klondike bar?
there is very little you would not do for a
Klondike bar.

Lay Down Memorial

Just lay down. Let me pull your
boxers down to your hernia scar,

the prettiest place on your body.
Make eye contact with your rougher down—

look at what you've made;
a lean, a symbol for itself.

I catch the image of you, and the other—
in the same Pompeii cast.

Ash and burns all over you both,
all over the bottoms of my tourist feet.

I lean back and look up at my ceiling
and decide whether or not to suck

you off. I'd like to, if only for the
peace, the quiet I am allowed when

my lips pull like a starving pig.
I don't have to look at you, I don't

have to be aware or involved,
Except of my hands and perhaps
my teeth.

Soda-jerk

1.) Just for the taste of it

Again, I dreamt about soda. In this episode
I watched while she rubbed her thumb,
index and middle fingers together,
wanting me to take what was left of
his paycheck after he got a discount.

2.) Always Coca-Cola

He brought the bottle and instructed.
That would kill the 67-year-old sperm,
if they were still kicking.

3.) Can't beat the real thing

She pulled my hair out of my face;
and I put the mouth of the 20oz coke inside me.

4.) Enjoy

It was an old wives tale, or midwives
or ex-wives tale, that had me in the tub
in three inches of water trying to flood him out.

5.) Diet Coke

One never knows where wisdom will fail.
It tastes just about the same going down.

He had a huge scar across his back

I tell them about the big guy, all 345 lbs, 6'2' of
him.
How he was a woodworker, a drummer.
I didn't leave out the part about his Dalmatian
two-toned penis.

How when he accidentally dumped in me when I
was blacked out—
I made him buy the morning after pill.
He wanted to see if he could be a dad.

I knew what that meant. It meant, *let me hold
myself, woman—*
let me hold myself and give it back
I'm intimately familiar with his simple tongue.

I'm familiar with lifting up the apron flap of
the man's stomach to expose his fleshy
browned mount and I didn't mind. Him crushing
down on me.

I am a strong girl, my thighs empires.
Let me be clear— I am all excess.
My hips indifferent to his enormity—
we could fuck, and it was fine.

I pulled his beard and slapped his face when he
asked.
He would choke me blue when I wanted that—
and when I asked him to cut me— he wouldn't.

That, as far as I could tell, was love:
A man who wouldn't draw blood
even if I asked.

Girls driving chariots

Early in the new century still,
they drove away everyday they could

through the mountains, the deserts
through Gallup towards Arizona.

When gas was an affordable blood
they went to Camel Back Mountain.

Under the passenger's seat slept an
8-inch buck knife, a gift from an older brother

for little girls on road trips.
And being that they were just that—

and high on prescribed Adderall
and pop and smokes and fear,

one girl grabbed the knife and held it out the window—
for all the potential rapists behind them to admire.

The other, explained to the police, what it means
to be high with a slit early in the new century.

That angel wasn't back-lit

He had a five o'clock shadow
long fingernails
a slight harelip

She dropped her jaw in disbelief
and the room began to close in
he brought her some water when
he saw she was about to faint

she thought how soft were those
filthy wings and the straw of that bed
needed changing— the water tasted funny
and the cattle were lowing

or was that the sound of her own
sweet soft hymn, familiar like
her migraines, the angel knew her
and delivered to her body

the message of hope, some life
and the burden of satisfaction

the withdrawal method

about as effective as a comma in stopping
a thought,
you, in-between my lesser angels.
We check afterward for your signature
if you signed off on the experience
or I did—
somewhere in the most daily of acts
a check cashed
I, we, wait a month to see if it clears

Jackie's Oh-face

What bottle blonde— pill loving— incest
survivor can compete with that?

thighs milky spindles
promised to a prince

who preferred more meat with his cake
than Oleg Cassini

Afraid to muss her hair, her pearls she was
frequently on top or backward cowgirl wearing
those cool sunglasses

of disinterest, hiding her wide set eyes
setting the bar for our mothers too high.

A Woman Sold Spices
(Bomdila Arunachal Pradesh)

lots of indigo

It was an imperfect pixilation on the
cover of the New York Times.

I don't read papers. I say I read them online,
but mostly I don't.

I saw a woman selling her spices gazing out
lightly over her dried ground
and wanted to write her down again—

give her another chance to make sense.
September 5th 2009

Her head cocked, early 40's— or early 30's
from a hard life and no access to lotions with
the latest fuzzy technologies—

The man on my bed is one I will find online.
The kind of organic meeting every young girl
dreams of.

Large hands deviated septum
scars from heart surgery and part of his colon
removed—

A pale strip of hairless skin around the finger
He had dedicated to his wife and three children.

(Continued on page 16)

And me 20 years behind him trying not to laugh
or die when he sucks too eagerly from my good
breast.

He can't decide whether to look at my report card
or
slam my legs behind my neck

I can see the way we look at each other— sizing
up empires
checking for weakness in the other's defense...
grazing— the minefields.

I should be sitting on an old mat letting my
leathery eyes
rest lightly over something else from this earth.

What to remember when walking behind a woman.
(What to remember when you are walked behind.)

If your footfall accelerates, so does her heartbeat.
She will remember what she learned in the 6th grade:

-Don't wear your ipod at night
-Don't walk home in heels.
-Don't have anything but your keys laced between your
        fingers
-Don't fiddle with your purse, or look down
-Don't fix your ponytail
-Don't walk on the unlit side of the street

-Keep your cell phone pre-dialed to 911
-Make sure your keychain is a heavy carabineer
-Find the houses with the lights on— yell fire
-Walk as if you have a big dick swinging between your
        hairless legs
-Walk with your footfall accelerating
-Walk as though you are looking for someone to hurt.

 And if they try and rape you,
-piss yourself
-make yourself puke

And if no one hears you,
-survive it.

They are drawn to the light, not the neck,[1]

I was cashing him out, and not feeling friendly
when the first bee of May _bombus apidae_
came between us. I didn't want to sleep with him
until he told me in a thick brogue,

they are attracted to movement
that even dogs when they attack
lunge for the light above the shoulder,
and not your neck[2]

Once, in a tunderstorm
I was out with another fella
carrying bails of straw
back to the burn

When the lightnin first littup,
rats came out of our bails
toward the light, they were all over us—[3]

I told the other guy to stay steady,
Just lettum run downya,
don't panic n- throw 'em, or lash out
that's when they bite.[4]

I opened the register and gave him his change.
The bee landed on my right breast
he laughed, and said _go easy gurl, let'tim pass._[5]

The bee flew off into the enormous front window
of the store, and as the man walked out the door
he turned and said
Good luck wid' him girl,
just keep still.[6]

[1]A girl can fill out her skeleton anyway she likes. Unless her thyroid is sluggish, or she spent too many hours under a plaid arm afraid to move— to offend. Then her bones are buried treasure, found under folds later in life when she and her spine lay back when asked.

[2]Every time you spread for so much as a tampon, you are brought back to that couch, the place you first learned to stay.

[3]You're fucked, and it keeps happening.

[4]After a certain point, it is just silly to remember. Event horizon flashes one last light, and anything can be boring.

[5]The Little Mermaid lost her voice when her legs split.

[6]Sometimes you hold your position when you are in danger, so the light around you doesn't invite invasion.

Ugly little life

I, Eros

lost my piercings
when I came to visit
you in prison.
I didn't even want to see you, but
I did want to see prison.
You hid your stash on
the Styrofoam ceiling
squares above my bed.

I made enough money
to cover your rent.
I enjoyed the safety
of your absence.

*****

I, Electra

hauled your
immensity back into bed
over piss jars,

scraped your lineage.
Please suspend the meter of this
particular sear. Forgive me.

I had to. I was prescripted against
life. Failed contract against yolk.

Do you remember loving me?
Cutting up your cigarettes?
Painting your toe nails?

I want to be in the back of your
car— freckled, eyes closed. Little
again sinking

to the bottom of some lake.

In the deer body

I was cold and walking
to the grocery store blocks away
when I saw her. I looked up and
saw her. Warm bleeding sagging thing.
Eyes already on fire with flies.
Sweet thing.

I pet her head kneeled next
to her, laid on my side and
spooned her as cars passed on.
I took out
my key and jammed it in between my sweet
thing's
shoulder blades and pulled down.

I pulled down with a sawing motion.
Until there was a gash long enough for me
to get my hands in and rip her to the tail.
Sweet spine, I took you out. After cracking
you away from legs and skull.

Fashioned a cross from the bones
and buried your heart, your brain
under your thoracic vertebrae *t*
held together with one of my shoelaces.

Venison scented skullcaps
dandybloom behind
the eyes I'm inside her the
elegant un-stag female thing
at the joints she's broken
and I marionette in her, of her
with her.

what that becomes

He turns on the tv to a commercial for Verizon.
She's a cheerleader for the Cowboys
on high definition— a commercial to
make you want that particular service.

When what you are servicing
is the desire the grab her by the waist
and split her in half
with those white boots still on.

Then, sweat and awkwardly climax
into that tan bone bag you push off yourself
cowgirl style,

and forget.

--

After your daydream, she picks herself up
wipes herself off
and begins again.

She finds a social worker,
tells her boss,
prepares the nest.

Her roots grow out and her ass widens
and flattens.

She decorates in soft pastels,
and gathers her aunts and step dad to gift her.

(Continued on page 24)

She collects her WIC and forgets her toenails.

She heats up a microwave dinner,
reapplies her chap stick
and turns on the tv.

Illegotcka[7]

Tying a bandana under
my hair—
Sloping home without my bra—
where the light is less—
Bed making in the morning is best.
It is important to have one thing I can un-do at night.

Shoulders curve under the purse, missing
essentials, to be searched for in vain after
the visit to Danny Moon.
He pays for company
in frozen cartons of Marlboros,
lives on his GI allowance.

His missing teeth, his toddler-wide smile— in Colorado,
letting his homeless friends
crash on his carpet, watching our conversation
and never contributing

The sleep has eased the tremor.
A sacrifice and some water, perhaps some bread and
a quick glance in the mirror confirms my
swollen over-eyes, and migrant mascara.
Alkásh[8]

sleep it off just sleep it off

shall we drink again bright angel?

[7]Neilegalnych, Polish for illegal, this title is Eng-olish
[8]Russian slang for alcoholic

I climb you

and stay for a minute
watch the alcohol leave my breath

everything about you is buryable
and jaw clenched you
can smell my switchback hips
on the sway—

a fucking.

I taste you hair products and
honey your wholeness swallows
and youth spits out half

I am letting you cradle me
with enough sun to make us
fill milk cartons with tears

when you touch my chest, the flat
space between my insistently uneven
breasts, I turn to water and pour.

emotional hemophiliac

my guardian angel
is eyeing up some other self-loather
with curvier, sexier problems
but still— I want to put my mouth on
your mouth— I want you to unzip my sternum

I want you to get in up to your elbows
and root around for the still born
break its legs if you must
just get it out of me

It is messy & the stitching will require focus
I will try and buck you off while you knot-tie
simple surgeon— your hands are delicate
enough to slow the bleeding

I like your face, your brow, certain of itself
your eyes always apologizing—
forgive me, understand I live both here
and there
one foot on my own throat
the other in the sea

Pub Sow

They put these long skinny silver
nipples on top of all the liquor.
It makes the pour smoother.
The rim of this particular bar—
a breached sow with articulated
teats, controlling the flow.

What do I have in common
with beautiful women?
There must be something besides
the sag that equalizes.
I have never had a figure.

I will never mourn the loss of one.
And still I take vitamins and hear
car horns and carry umbrellas as if
the abacus in my spleen is counting
down to the great cellular
release, the pour of internal
pudding— the bloat of death.
I will swell unless burned...
even then I will blow, and lose nothing
I never had.

Acknowledgements

rats in the grass and *priority* published in *Ditch* 2009

Silver reasonably priced wine opener published in
The Common Ground summer 2011

After hours off the cross published in *Confrontation*

Belly fat not child published in *Stymie*

Special Thanks to:

April Bernard
Amy Gerstler
Mark Wunderlich
Ed Ochester
Elizabeth Witte **(massive thanks for the title!)**
Shawna Kay Rodenberg
Dana Brigham
Mark Pearson
Katie McCarthy
Nick Forti
Evan & Rebecca Perriello
Paul Theriault
Jessica Foley
Gordon Purkis for supporting my work. (I'm
so grateful.)
My family: Lan- Elizabeth- Mike & my meat pies.
Most especially my mother Christine,
who will blush and tell her friends not to read this.